The Tally Man

Rita Jerram

Stairwell Books //

Published by Stairwell Books and Fighting Cock Press
161 Lowther Street
York, YO31 7LZ
and
2, Pinfold Close,
Riccall,
York
YO19 6QZ

www.stairwellbooks.co.uk
@stairwellbooks

The Tally Man © 2022 Rita Jerram, Stairwell Books and Fighting Cock Press

All rights reserved. No part of this publication may be reproduced, stored in or introduced into a retrieval system, or transmitted, in any form, or by any means (electronic, mechanical, photocopying, recording, e-book or otherwise) without the prior written permission of the author.

The moral rights of the author have been asserted.

Any person who does any unauthorised act in relation to this publication may be liable to criminal prosecution and civil claims for damages. Purchase of this book in e-book format entitles you to store the original and one backup for your own personal use; it may not be resold, lent or given away to other people and it may only be purchased from the publisher or an authorised agent. This book is sold subject to the condition that it shall not, by way of trade or otherwise, be lent, resold, hired out, or otherwise circulated without the author's prior consent in any form of binding or cover other than that in which it is published and without a similar condition including this condition being imposed on the subsequent purchaser

Edited: Pauline Kirk and Caitlin Brown
Layout: Alan Gillott and Caitlin Brown
Cover design: Alan Gillott and Caitlin Brown

ISBN: 978-1-913432-10-2

Also by Rita Jerram

Tales From a Prairie Journal

A Shadow in My Life

Editors' Note

The original manuscript of *The Tally Man* consisted of 17 chapters, arranged in the order in which Rita had written them. Some included duplicate versions, apparently shortened to read to a group. Though unfinished and surviving only in a single typescript, Rita's vivid writing and the historical interest of her account of a vanished world, made it well worth sharing.

We have removed repetitions where necessary and smoothed some of the roughness of Rita's writing – this was clearly an unpolished draft – but otherwise kept alterations to a minimum. Rather than add an ending, we have rearranged the sketches to give a chronological development, and to end with Rita's own words. Each sketch can be read alone, however, as it deals with a different aspect of her father's life.

Despite being a challenging project, it has been a privilege to help preserve a delightful memoir.

Pauline Kirk and Caitlin Brown

To all the ordinary women who create the extraordinary

Table of Contents

A Mismatch 1

Love from Mother: My Father's Youth 6

A Gift of Life 11

Brothers 15

The Club 18

Goose Grease and Whiskey 21

The German Invasion 24

Holiday of a Lifetime 28

Money Talks 32

Sabotage 36

The Illuminations 38

A Dog's Life 40

The Money Bag 44

The Valley That Died 47

The Boxing Day Hunt 52

The Mistress 55

A Family Reunion 58

A Mismatch

My elder sister was conceived one foggy autumn night in a gloomy Birmingham lodging house. It's possible that if the weather had been kinder, she might never have been born, nor myself or the three sisters who followed later.

My mother until that time had imagined herself in love with a 'Midland Red' bus driver, although not entirely convinced that it was reciprocated. He had never asked her out, but he always sounded his horn when passing her house, which being on a return service route was beginning to annoy the neighbours.

My father was a peddler who came to be known as the 'Tally Man'. He was well known and respected in the mining village where my mother had lived all her life. He travelled there each week with his stock of Sheffield stainless steel cutlery and gold jewellery. My maternal grandmother had been tempted a few months earlier by a shiny set of his cutlery, laid out on blue velvet and arranged in a polished box with brass clasps. The persuasive peddler had convinced her that she could afford to own it. "Just a small deposit," he had told her, and he would call every week for the next year to collect her further payments. She would never use it, preferring her old yellowing knife and forks that were in daily use. It would go into the china cabinet along with the unused half china tea-set with rosebuds on, that had been a wedding present from her parents.

Every Friday evening, punctual at 6pm, my father would rap on the door calling, "Good evening, it's the Tally Man." My grandmother would reach for the payment card and his sixpence kept under an ornament on the mantelpiece, and whilst my father dealt with the paperwork she would take one of her better cups and saucers from the sideboard and pour him a cup of tea from a pot stewing on the hearth. An occupational hazard of Tally men was that ever ready cup of stewed tea.

My mother usually came home at about this time, tired and dusty from her nine-hour shift at the local pottery, where for the last four years she had packed crockery into straw lined crates. She was a fresh-faced buxom girl, rather timid and reserved, quite unlike her younger sister who was bold and vivacious. Her biggest adventure to that date, had been a week's holiday in Blackpool the previous summer with two friends from work. She shyly showed the Tally Man the photograph of the three girls all giggling in embarrassment at being snapped wearing their modest bathing suits. He politely, but with little interest glanced at it, and continued whilst sipping his hot tea to talk of his plans to expand his business. He said he needed to employ a young lady to assist him, his original choice being my mother's sister, whose bright personality seemed best suited to the work. She was keen at first, but on discovering that the position entailed some evening work quickly changed her mind, not prepared to give up the pleasures of the local dance hall.

My mother nervously spoke up and said she would like to be considered for the job. Having been good at arithmetic at school she felt she could manage the financial side of the position, and was willing to learn the art of salesmanship. With the promise of the same weekly wage she was already earning, and a possible rise after three months, she shook hands with the Tally Man and accepted his offer.

My mother loved her new employment and took to the Tally Man's business with an enthusiasm to match his own. She became adept at appraising potential customers for their worth and honesty, both important factors in the credit industry, and once she had got over her initial shyness she enjoyed riding alongside him in his car. Seeing her former work-mates trudging home from the pottery gave her a warm feeling of superiority. She was a business girl now.

Two evenings a week were devoted to finding new customers to extend the already flourishing credit rounds. Choosing unexplored areas my mother and her new employer would knock on doors showing prospective customers the range of goods they carried with them in large leather bags, their newest line proving popular. Every household was keen to have a beautiful walnut encased chiming clock in pride of place on their sideboards. They often worked late, my mother returning home flushed with the success of their endeavours. Her parents were at first a little dubious about their daughter working in such close proximity with the Tally Man especially the late evening work she was expected to do. But they reasoned that she was not yet eighteen and unlikely to harbour romantic notions about a man touching forty, despite his charm and well set up appearance, and anyway it was common knowledge that he was living in sin with a woman in the next town.

A few months after my mother had started working for him, the Tally Man decided to extend his business to cover the thriving industrial areas of Birmingham, and within weeks had built up a sizeable credit round. The housewives of the 'Black Country' were just as eager to own a few luxuries as the miners' wives of South Derbyshire. It became a regular weekly visit to the smoke blackened terraces and tenements to collect his payments, my mother's kidneys adjusting in time to the inevitable and innumerable cups of strong tea.

On one such visit in mid-winter, a sudden fierce snowstorm engulfed them on their homeward journey, making it impossible to travel and forcing them to find lodgings for the night in Birmingham. My mother's parents spent a frantic night worrying about their absent daughter. On her return the next morning any anxieties they had felt about her physical or moral danger were soon expelled by her explanation, accepting it would have been foolhardy to travel in such weather, my grandmother's only comment being the hope that the sheets were clean and properly aired, having no trust in unknown boarding houses, especially in Birmingham. The second occasion that my mother failed to return home was a night when most of middle England was engulfed by a dense choking fog. Her parents were not so worried this time and slept soundly, knowing their daughter's welfare would be well taken care of by the Tally Man.

The results of his tender care became obvious six weeks later, when my mother discovered she was pregnant. Ashamed, she told her parents. They were shocked and angry at her employer's duplicity. The next time the Tally Man called to collect my mother for work he was surprised to be invited in and ushered into the parlour. He was equally horrified at the news, not intending his dalliance to have such consequences, but sitting at my grandmother's highly polished table facing the wrath of my mother's parents, and seeing the anger and threatening eyes of her four grown brothers, he had little option other than to propose marriage to her.

Despite a liking for women, wedded bliss had never been part of his future plans. He had always taken his pleasures in the safe company of married women, having occasional liaisons with some of his more accommodating female customers. But he accepted his fate manfully and married my mother the following week by special licence, his only condition being the insistence that it would be an early morning ceremony, the afternoon and evening would be work as usual for both of them.

Seven months later my sister was born, and my father was overjoyed.

My parents were totally unsuited, only finding unity in the business in which my mother became invaluable, but sadly their marriage lacked warmth. I often wondered if she might have been happier with her bus driver.

Love from Mother: My Father's Youth

The day that Queen Victoria died had a profound effect on my father's life, no fault of her Majesty; it was the day his mother chose to leave his father and end her marriage. He was unaware at the time of her momentous decision, being not yet three years old and still in short frocks.

His parent's union had started with passion, but ended in strife. His mother a well-educated and sophisticated young woman, had the misfortune, as she later realised, to fall in love with her father's groom. Being a passionate and self-willed girl, she had disobeyed her parents and run off with the good-looking servant.

Ten years later she found herself living in poor circumstances, and the handsome groom no longer quite so appealing. He had become a bully and was portraying a growing fondness for alcohol. The fact that she had lived to regret her headstrong elopement, thus fulfilling her father's prophecy, was of little comfort, as by this time she had four children, the youngest being a new-born baby.

On her father's death a few months earlier, she had been left a monthly allowance, a mere pittance compared to her brother's inheritance; he had received the bulk of their father's fortune. But the monthly sum had eased the grief of her long estrangement from her family, with the knowledge that her father had not entirely cast her off despite threatening to do so.

The allowance gave her the power to do what had seemed impossible before, and taking only her new-born son she fled. Sympathetic neighbours cared for the three forsaken children whilst their father scoured the town for any sign of his errant wife. He heard rumours that she had journeyed to Liverpool, and from there set sail for Canada. His anger was increased by the realisation that her monthly income had also gone with her, and he could no longer rely on its contribution to finance his growing dependence on alcohol.

Cap in hand he visited his wife's affluent relatives to request help for his deserted brood, and possibly some monetary recompense to make amends for his own devalued status. His wife's childless brother offered to take the two elder girls into his home, willing to nurture and educate them as if his own. They grew up in luxury, with servants and a carriage at their beck and call, and later attended finishing schools in France, eventually both marrying men of substance.

My father, a forlorn little boy bewildered by the turn of events, was not included in this good fortune, not finding the favour in his aunt's eyes that his two sisters had. His father had been given a generous sum of money by his brother-in-law, attained by a promise not to contact his daughters or their new family again. Bitter and angry at his wife's desertion he decided to leave the area and returned to the rural district where he was born taking his remaining child, my father, with him.

Fortunately, he purchased a small farm with the bulk of the money before drowning his sorrows with ale. Over a period of time his bitterness and deep resentment resulted in him becoming known as a heavy drinking, bad tempered recluse who shunned any social contact.

My father, who had very little memory of his mother or siblings was mainly ignored. His pre-school days were spent on the isolated farm, his childish needs met by a farm labourer's wife from the nearest village. She was not a motherly woman. Thin faced and gaunt of figure, she came daily to clean and supposedly attend the young child's welfare. She would snarl at him and often beat his frail little body, punishing him unnecessarily, venting her own life's frustrations on him. When his bruises became noticeable, even to his father's uncaring eyes, she was dismissed, and another kindlier villager employed. My father always remembered this woman. She gave him a brief glimpse of warmth and affection. She felt sorry for the 'little mite' as she called him, and unpicked her old jumpers to knit Jerseys for him and sat him on her knee for cuddles. But she too left; when protesting to his father about the 'little mite's' neglect she was verbally abused and ordered off the farm.

Despite these misfortunes my father reached school age: a sturdy little boy who seldom talked, never smiled, and found his comfort with the farm animals, or in the open countryside where he roamed freely with only a dog as his companion. His father took him to the village school the first day, instructing the teacher to cane the child as much as was needed to rid him of any badness. The next day he had to find his own way there and back, six miles in all. The village women muttered about the state of the boy and wondered how a father could send a child to school so ill clad, an old cut-down shirt and torn trousers, no warm jacket to face the cold winter mornings, and often no 'snap box' for his lunch. Kindly women who could ill afford it themselves, gave him a hot pasty or a slice of freshly baked bread when he passed their door. These were the few treats that my father long remembered.

His life on the farm with his father was stark. They went to bed at dusk and rose again at daybreak. Sometimes his father would fall into a black mood, locking himself away with drink for days and nights, coming out eventually to stare at his small son as if unaware of who he was. At these times my father would rise early and quietly attend to the farm chores, feeding the animals, milking their cow, drinking the warm milk straight from the pail, searching for newly laid eggs in the barn, and then, lighting a fire in the old kitchen range he would cook himself fried eggs for breakfast.

If late for school he would take a short cut, crossing the river could save him an extra mile. One wet day he slipped on the moss-covered stepping-stones falling into the fast flowing swollen river. He was saved by a sharp eyed poacher who, returning home alongside the riverbank, saw the boy slip and raced forward in time to fish him out. My father shaking, and still choking with the water he'd swallowed, and his over large boots squelching with mud, arrived at school five minutes late and was soundly caned for it, and then sent back home to change his clothes. On arrival at the farm his father thrashed him for missing school, not stopping to listen to his tale.

Christmas or birthdays were not recognised by his father, they were just another day with work to be done. My father never forgot the day he received the postcard from Canada. On one side there was a picture of the Rocky Mountains, on the other his name and address and the words 'LOVE FROM MOTHER'. He carried it around with him for a long time, occasionally taking it from his pocket to look at the picture of the rugged mountain range, to study the colourful Canadian stamp and to move his finger over and over those magic words. He fell asleep every night repeating them and slept with the postcard under his pillow. It was the only contact his mother ever made.

Despite my father's neglected childhood and loveless upbringing, he grew up to be a caring responsible adult, who could be forgiven a little wildness in his youth and his occasional outbursts of rage. His harrowing past gave him a burning desire to make something of his life, to be self-sufficient and to answer to no one.

He was a warm loving father to my sisters and me. After he had died, I was sorting his effects and I found tucked away at the back of his desk an old cigar box. Inside was every birthday card we had ever sent him, and at the bottom wrapped in tissue paper a yellowing crumbling postcard, the Rockies now a faint blur and the faded writing unclear but just legible enough to read the word 'MOTHER'.

I wept then for my father and also that sad lonely little boy who only had a postcard to love.

A Gift of Life

But for the refusal of a twenty-pound loan, my father's life might have taken a totally different direction, and consequently he would have not spent the next seventy years with a bullet hole in his calf, which caused him considerable pain in damp weather.

He was just sixteen years of age in 1914 when England declared war on Germany. Initially the onset of the First World War did little to disturb the tranquillity of the peaceful countryside where he lived, other than a few local village boys who seeking excitement and adventure took the King's Shilling and enlisted. It had no impact on my father. Still sharing an uneasy existence with his father on their isolated farm, he was more concerned with making a living.

Since leaving school three years earlier, he had managed to save a small sum of money, mostly earned by hiring out his labour to neighbouring farmers and being a strong willing lad, he had always found plenty of eager employers. Despite working long hours, he still did his unpaid chores for his father, for which he received his meagre bed and board.

When his savings were adequate, he invested in a milking cow, first gaining his father's reluctant permission to allow him to graze it in their bottom meadow. This became the first of my father's many business ventures. He would rise early, milk his cow, and then walk the three miles into the nearest village carefully carrying the pail of creamy, still warm milk. Consistent timing, plus his shy smile and handsome face, soon established a regular custom, allowing him the notion of purchasing a second cow. But his enterprise was curbed when his father refused permission to allow any more cows on his pastures. Determined that his venture would succeed my father persuaded an elderly local farmer to sell him a small field. To complete this purchase he needed twenty pounds, being that much short of the asking price. His father rejected his plea for a temporary loan. So, at daybreak the following day my father set off to walk the twelve miles to the nearest town, determined to seek a bank loan. He was rebuffed at every bank he tried. His youth and lack of parental support made him a poor risk in the eyes of the careful bank managers he saw.

It was a dejected and bitter young man who started his long walk back home. Two miles out of town he passed the newly built army barracks, a hive of activity as raw young recruits were being prepared for war. He saw Lord Kitchener's poster on the wall. It seemed to be pointing directly at him. 'Your Country Needs You' it said. On impulse he turned and headed back to town. At the temporary recruiting office he added another year to his age and signed up, becoming a private in His Majesty's army. He was given twenty-four hours to settle his affairs before reporting to the barracks for his initial training.

He hitched a lift back to the village on a farm wagon, and when the driver heard of his enlistment, he offered to buy my father's milking cow. With his business matters arranged my father only had to say his farewells at home. His father turned away when told of his son's future plans. "Do as you please, it's of no interest to me," he replied.

Two days later my father was in a khaki uniform and off to the Yorkshire Moors for six weeks basic training. Before leaving he had found time to use his cash from the sale of the cow to purchase a bulk supply of tobacco, assuming it would reap a good profit from his fellow recruits whilst in the wilds of Yorkshire.

My father was a loner, not accustomed to the company of his contemporaries, but he quickly established himself as a purveyor of tobacco and occasional financial loans, always making sure of a good interest rate on the re-payments. When shipped to France six weeks later he had already made a profit and was able to open his first bank account.

He never talked about his early experiences in the trenches, but the re-occurring nightmares that he suffered over the next seven decades said it all. When his rural background became known he was transferred to the stable units. His new duties were equally dangerous but more to his liking. He groomed and cared for the horses by day, but when nightfall came his job was to move forward the heavy guns to new positions. The guns were pulled through the mud-churned French soil by the horses, my father guiding them to an appointed spot. Across the open stretch of countryside known as 'No Man's Land' he often saw his German counterpart doing likewise.

One moonlit night, whilst positioning the heavy gun, he heard a whistle and soft call and realised it was directed at him from across the open land. The whistle was repeated again, this time seeming nearer, and then a shadowy figure appeared at the edge of a clump of trees nearby. The two soldiers stared at each other for a full minute, my father seeing a scrawny young fellow who looked even younger than himself, whose overcoat and helmet overpowered his frail body. He laid his rifle on the ground and advanced towards my father with his hand held out. It was the nearest my father had been to a German and he had not expected to see a lad who looked like any of the village youths back home. He walked fearfully forward to meet him, and when both reached a halfway point they stopped, taking stock of each other before offering a tentative handshake. The German made a gesture to indicate he would like to smoke, but then shook his head and pointed to his empty pockets. My father realised he was asking for a cigarette, and he offered one of his which was gratefully accepted with renewed handshaking and a beaming smile. They sat on a small bank amongst the trees and smoked in a comfortable silence, and then once again shook hands, slapped each other on the back, and returned to their respective sides.

A few nights later when my father was once more bringing the big gun forward, he saw the German boy again, standing by a fringe of trees on the far edge of the enemy lines. My father waved and strode forward to meet him, but too late saw the German officer standing behind his clandestine smoking partner, hidden at first by an overhanging branch. My father was rooted to the spot when the young soldier raised the rifle and pointed it directly at his heart, and on a harsh command he fired...at my father's ankle.

The war was now over for him. He spent six months in a military hospital giving him plenty of time to reflect on the German soldier's look of anguish when ordered to fire on him, and the realisation that the only time in his life that he had given away tobacco free of charge had most probably saved his life.

He was discharged from the army as an invalid and sent to a convalescent home on the south coast. When fully recovered he decided not to return to his father's farm. His healthy bank account and his newly acquired taste for travel decided him to broaden his horizons.

Brothers

In 1922 my father was deported from Canada and forcibly returned to England. This deportation caused a serious sixty-year feud between my father and his younger brother Arnold.

They had been happily reunited only three years earlier, having been parted as children when their parents separated. Arnold had been taken to Canada by their mother, and my father was left in the care of his father on a remote farm in Derbyshire where he grew up a lonely and neglected child. At his earliest opportunity he had left the farm, enlisting in the army, and fighting in the First World War. In 1919, after recovering from wounds received in France, and the war at an end, my father took passage to Canada, hoping to find his mother and brother.

He eventually traced them to Vancouver, finding his mother with a new partner, and none too pleased to have this strapping son who closely resembled her deserted husband knocking at the door. But his brother was delighted to see him and, after a heartening reunion, they decided to take advantage together of land that was being offered cheaply by the Canadian government, and using my father's savings they purchased a large tract of land in British Columbia close to the American border.

They grew sweetcorn and watermelons and ran a few hundred cattle. They worked hard and played hard, drinking their own whiskey made from a home-made still. They socialised with Indians on a nearby reservation who would sell their souls for alcohol. Life for the two of them was good.

Then they had a couple of bad seasons with poor crops and little grass for the cattle. Money was short and the brothers were worried about their future.

Their farm was saved by the announcement of Prohibition in America. They went full-time into the 'Moonshine' business, more stills were made, and their illegal whiskey production was on its way. They had become 'bootleggers'.

The end product would be loaded on to a wagon and driven through the night and across the American border. They always drove to the border disguised as a courting couple. Arnold, being the smaller and daintier of the two, would drape a shawl over his head and nestle close to my father who held the horses' reins with one hand and placed his other arm protectively around his so-called 'sweetheart', giving the impression of a loving couple.

Their underhand trading became more lucrative than farming. They were making small fortunes, buying more land, both investing in the latest American Cadillac.

All went well until the night my father drove across the border alone, whilst Arnold was sleeping off the effects of his own extra potent 'Moonshine'. He arrived early at the pre-arranged location and waited uneasily with his wagon load of liquor for the handover to take place. The expected Yankee contacts turned out to be plain clothes police officers acting on a tip off. My father was arrested, spending two nights in prison before being handed over to the Canadian Mounties who promptly deported him back to England.

He never saw or heard from his brother again. He made many attempts to return to Canada, twice trying to slip in over the American border and once using a false passport, but he was not successful. He was desperate for his share of their combined wealth, but letters to his brother were returned many months later, stamped 'address unknown'.

Eventually my father realised the futility of his pursuit and resigned himself to staying in England and starting again from scratch.

He vowed vengeance on his brother and threatened to kill him on sight for his betrayal. It was the betrayal more than the loss of money that angered him the most. He would have found some way to have given Arnold his share if their roles had been reversed, my father being an honest rogue.

He held this vendetta for sixty years and carried it to his grave.

Two years after my father's death Uncle Arnold visited England a wealthy, respectable rancher from Alberta. He visited my father's grave to make his peace.

A little late I thought.

The Club

My father, by birth and inclination, was of a farming background, but in the 1920s when family circumstances forced a change of career, he became a pedlar (sometimes known as the 'Tally Man'). He hauled his packs of cutlery, wedding rings and pocket watches door to door across the towns and countryside of South Derbyshire. Slowly, with hard work and quality goods he was able to build up a sizeable credit round. Many households in that area are still cutting their bread with one of my father's Sheffield steel bread knives, and a few ageing ladies still proudly wear the gold wedding rings on their swollen fingers that my father sold them for sixpence down and sixpence a week.

Many of his customers in South Derbyshire were miners. "The Salt of the Earth," he called them, never missing a weekly payment. He gained their respect and loyalty by not calling when they were off sick or out on strike. But such was their calibre they always caught up with back payments as soon as they returned to work. Not all were so honest, and old miners still remember talk of one who was put upside down in his own rainwater butt by my father for disputing his account.

In the 1930s he became more ambitious and rented shop premises, branching out with furniture, carpets and lino. The family still have some of his original pre-war advertising leaflets which offered a complete home of furniture for young newlyweds, of bedroom suite, dining set and two fireside chairs, plus a free mat of the bride's choice. All this for a special price of twelve guineas, five shillings deposit required and weekly repayments of half a crown.

My father worked long hours and built a prosperous family business. His rivals were the 'Jays' and 'Cantors', multiple furnishing companies of the High Street. But his customers trusted him for his fairness and solid hard-wearing goods and stayed loyal. In the 1950s he ventured almost by accident into a different line of business, becoming a licensed money lender. At this time washing machines were becoming popular, so he sold off his stock of dolly pegs and mangles and invested in a load of machines. These were soon in demand by his regular customers, but at this stage he hit a snag. The government of the time were insisting on a 25% deposit on all electrical goods and this was hard to find. So, my father had the idea of lending the customer the deposit money, which was then handed back to him, covering the legal requirements. His faithful customers came to appreciate this extra service he was providing, and his new business venture expanded. They borrowed each year for their week's holiday in Blackpool or Skegness, sometimes calling to collect the money on their way to the station, suitcases in hand. Housewives borrowed to clear debts they didn't want their husbands to know about. And once we had a bride come to the door in bridal gown and veil, still clutching her wilting bouquet, asking for a loan to pay for the honeymoon.

Despite paying interest of fifteen shillings on every five pounds borrowed, my father's customers thought of it as a club where you paid your weekly subs and got your dividends when required. Old established customers would introduce relatives or friends eager to join. My father was very astute, always knowing when to say no.

His business was unique, impossible to imagine in these days of plastic cards and high finance. He worked until his death at 84 years, still collecting his weekly rounds, an established, respected figure in many homes.

He had realised his dream of going back to his roots and combined his business with farming. Three generations of family customers came to pay their respects when he died, mourning a friend and the loss of their 'club'.

Goose Grease and Whiskey

I was born the runt of the litter and not expected to live, but I had one advantage over other runts – my father: a giant of a man who ploughed his straight furrows the old-fashioned way with a hand plough, and who built the best haystacks in our shire.

He had a lifetime distrust of the medical profession, a legacy of his time spent wounded in a military hospital during the first World War.

He was before his time with his knowledge and use of alternative medicine. More importantly, he was stubborn and had made up his mind that this runt was going to survive. He firmly believed that what worked on his beasts would work on me.

His first move was to buy a Jersey cow (at great expense, as he often told me in later years). She was kept tethered in our kitchen garden, producing gallons of rich, creamy milk twice a day. This in turn was pumped into me with great success – I started to thrive. Unfortunately I thrived too well and became, at ten months, a jowly heavyweight, too fat to be called a bouncy baby.

The inevitable happened – I became bronchial, with regular bronchitis attacks, but there was no great panic; my father had a secret weapon to deal with any such emergency – GOOSE GREASE. The yearly rendering of our Christmas goose made sure that my father always had a never-ending supply at hand. My fat little chest was plastered with it night and day for the next ten years. I wore it sandwiched between my vest and liberty bodice, freely spread on a piece of flannel. Worse was to follow – when I became old enough for school, I had to wear my goose grease armour every day, and goose grease, to put it nicely, STINKS – I was never very popular at school.

My father always insisted it was curing me, pointing out that I had suffered no bronchial attacks for years. My flannel bodyguard was obviously doing its work. Incidentally, my father had found another use for this precious grease. He was convinced it was a cure for hair loss. He proved that a nightly massage with it produced, eventually, a slight fuzz of hair on his own bald head. Who knows, a clever business plan might have made his fortune.

His home-made raspberry syrup was my favourite remedy, a delicious soothing linctus for sore throats, brought out at the first sneeze or sign of a cold. Unfortunately, it was quickly followed by an extra plastering of goose grease. "Just in case," my father said.

Being a runt, I often suffered bad ear infections and, of course, my father had a cure. He made little flannel bags filled with salt and warmed them on the kitchen range and pressed them tight against my ears to ease the pain.

My father's special, secret weapon was malt whiskey, his cure for all ills. A teaspoonful of whiskey with sugar and hot water, was the treatment for almost everything I suffered. I came to like it and often suffered on purpose for this pleasurable cure. The only time he gave in and allowed conventional medicine a chance was when he nearly lost me with pneumonia. After an anxious day and night by my bedside and with my temperature rising, he agreed to call in a doctor who brought with her a new wonder drug called Penicillin, although, my father did later take the credit for my recovery, having slipped some goose grease on my chest before the doctor arrived.

He got his way – I survived his ministrations and have lived to get my pension. However, on reflection, I sometimes think that the real magic of his medicine were the strong arms that held me and his blind faith in my survival.

The German Invasion

My father was always blamed, rather unfairly I thought, for the Germans' arrival in our rural backwater, and for the consequences of their brief stay in the area.

During that last summer of the Second World War when manpower was short, with most of the village men in the forces, local farmers were offered the labours of German prisoners of war who were being held at a camp in nearby Stafford. The idea was not generally popular in our parochial district, but much to the scorn of our neighbouring farmer John Fairclough, whose family had farmed 'Hill-Top Farm' for generations, my father had decided to accept the government's offer of much needed help with his haymaking.

In due course he drove to the camp and selected six young German prisoners, the only cost being their food and transport each day, plus their elderly guard who on arrival at the farm promptly fell asleep under a tree.

The boys, which is all they were, seemed a mixed bunch with not a farmer amongst them, but all eager to please and happy to leave the camp confines, despite the hard labour on offer.

A tall, good-looking, blonde boy called Karl became their spokesman having had a few years of learning English at school. They all worked hard and were glad of a respite at lunchtime, tucking into home cured ham generously spread with mustard, the mustard being my mother's concession to the German palate. This was followed by homemade cake washed down with plentiful mugs of tea. They were well satisfied when my father gave each of them a cigarette from his hoarded supply. By now a feeling of comradeship had prevailed and out came tattered photographs of loved ones back home, mothers and sweethearts, the boys brushing away tears when carefully returning them to their pockets. Karl said his family had all been killed in a bombing raid on Frankfurt, and he had no mementoes.

Soon the hot sun and good food took its toll and eyes started to close. They were rudely awakened by a loud voice from the other side of the hedge, shouting, "Murdering Sods!" It was our neighbour John Fairclough scything his hay in an adjoining field with his exhausted wife and daughter trailing behind him, raking and stacking sheaves from early morning till dusk. He was angrily swinging his scythe through the long grass as if seeing a German behind every blade.

My father, ignoring his remark and proximity, roused up the boys and all returned to their haymaking. It was noticeable that Karl worked close to the hedge-side where young Linda Fairclough was raking in the next field. She was a pretty girl, the only child and the apple of her father's eyes. She was aware of the young German's admiring glances, and could not resist smiling back, potential good-looking young men none too plentiful at that time. Noticing this interplay, her father ordered her to rake on the other side of the field.

The German boys worked so well that my father asked if two could become permanent, at least until winter came. He was given Karl and a quiet sullen boy called Erich. They came every day and were returned to the camp by my father each evening, often late if the farm work was extended. No guard was required as they were released on my father's assurances.

Linda, our neighbour's daughter, used to fetch their cows from the top fields every afternoon for milking, returning them early evening. Karl usually found a reason to be working in that vicinity at these times, and soon became good friends with her, my father turning a blind eye to his occasional absenteeism.

Without any prior warning the prison camp was closed, the Germans moved further south, and no more was heard of the two boys.

A few months later Linda Fairclough gave birth to a beautiful, blonde, blue-eyed baby. A virgin birth according to John Fairclough.

The war ended, the village men started to return home, and the farming community settled back to its pre-war rustic peace. One spring morning Karl walked up our farm lane. He had not gone back to Germany with the other repatriated prisoners; he had been working on a farm in the south of England since his release. He had come back for Linda not knowing he had a six months old son.

John Fairclough threw Linda and baby out of his home when Karl asked his permission to marry her, saying, "Take your whore and her Nazi brat and go back to Germany."

For the next two years Karl, Linda and baby Hans lived in a caravan bought by my father and placed in a corner of our farmyard. Karl worked hard becoming a very capable and efficient farm worker. Baby Hans often waved his fat chubby hand at the old man on his tractor in the next field, but John Fairclough never acknowledged him back. He died of a sudden heart attack when Hans was two and a half years old, never having spoken to his daughter again, and still blaming my father every night in the local pub for bringing the Germans to the village.

After his funeral Linda's mother came to the caravan to beg Linda, Karl and little Hans to move in with her and help to run the farm.

My father lamented that he had lost the best worker he'd ever had. But 'Hill-Top Farm' eventually, on Linda's mother's death, gained a new owner, and became for evermore known as the 'German's Place'.

Holiday of a Lifetime

My father never took a holiday, having no desire to leave his business or farm. He always said his travelling days were over. He generously sent the rest of us away for two weeks each summer, managing quite happily on his own. I think he secretly enjoyed that yearly break from family life. But in 1946, the year after the Second World War ended, he was faced with a dilemma – the doctor had advised that I needed sea air. Always a sickly child, a recent bout of bronchitis had left me very weak and pale. The obvious escort, my mother, was at that time very advanced with her third pregnancy and was unable to travel.

My father, after much deliberation and with many misgivings, agreed to take my sister and I for a short holiday. For some obscure reason he opted for Guernsey, one of the Channel Islands. In retrospect it was an odd choice to visit a small island only recently vacated by its German occupiers, and which at that time had little to recommend it as a suitable holiday destination for two small girls.

I have little memory of our actual departure, other than many last-minute instructions to my mother, who was left with the awesome responsibility of keeping the business intact. I remember that my father was dressed as if for a usual day at his office; sombre navy three-piece suit with his gold watch and chain fastened across the waistcoat, and his new black leather boots. So, with my mother's cautions ringing in our ears and with no sense of joy, we set off for our holiday.

We were to fly to the Island, a rare mode of travel at this time. Our flight was a private charter and departed from a small local aerodrome which had once been part of a large wartime R.A.F. base. It was now a newly ventured flying club operated single-handedly by a redundant fighter pilot. The aircraft was small with only four seats and no luxury fittings. We were the only passengers and soon became acquainted with the pilot who was sitting in front of us. He skilfully flew the plane whilst juggling with his navigation notes, and at the same time holding a long conversation with my father. He said he had never actually flown to Guernsey before and enlisted our help in locating key landmarks. Flying low, we were able to note necessary church spires, rivers and suchlike, and most important of all, Bournemouth pier which was his signal for a right hand turn out to sea. Despite being so occupied he still found time to hand out barley sugar and cotton wool when we complained of earache. The noise was deafening, our seats hard and uncomfortable, but we were flying, an unbelievable experience for my sister and me. During the journey I was sick twice, but my father just continued to look out to sea, believing such unpleasant happenings were best ignored.

Four hours later we arrived in St Peter's Port. It was pouring with rain and very cold. Our lodgings were in a tall gloomy terraced house overlooking the wharf. An equally gloomy landlady met us at the door and issued firm instructions as to our behaviour whilst on her premises. After demanding our ration books, she took us up the dark staircase to our rooms which were all painted in depressing dark green distemper. My sister and I burst into tears, upon which my father said goodnight and made a hasty exit.

Following our landlady's strict rules, we had to vacate the premises at 9am each day. I firmly believe that we were the only visitors on the island that week - the local population went about their business with no thoughts of future tourism. Each morning we walked aimlessly around the town, we girls hurrying to keep up with our father's brisk pace. Our wanderings took us past the many defence fortifications that the Germans had built after their invasion. They were stark and ugly, and dominated the skyline. To escape the rain, we ate our picnic lunch inside one of these monstrous bunkers and looking out to sea through the narrow slits I imagined a German soldier pointing his gun towards England. I felt a shiver down my spine. Young as I was, I could appreciate how awful it must have been to have lived on the Island under its recent occupation.

Our only diversion on these morning walks was the elderly lady who mistook my father's upright bearing and clipped tones for Germanic ancestry and tried to beat him round the head with her umbrella. Whenever we saw her approaching, my father forgot his dignity and ran, with his two giggling daughters close behind. Our afternoons were spent sitting on a rackety old bus whilst it covered its circular island route, exciting the first day, but decidedly tedious by the fifth. Promptly at 5pm we alighted outside the Clock Cafe in time for tea. The cafe's limited post-war menu became a daily challenge; the choice of Welsh rarebit or pilchards on toast was not inspiring. My sister and I soon realised that food was not the attraction that had led my father into such a dreary establishment. The smiling blonde waitress was the certain draw. She hovered about him and, when bending low to take our order, showed a wide expanse of her ample bosom. As well as her obvious sexual charms she usually managed to find an egg for his toast. He always went back to the cafe for a night-cap after putting us to bed.

On the first day of our holiday my father purchased a small red notebook, and every expenditure was carefully noted down in it on a daily basis: 3 Eldorado choc-ices 1/6d; bus fares 2/3d; teas at the Clock Café 7/6d and I could only presume that sundries 5/ was the night he took the blonde waitress to the pictures, but never dared asked him.

With much relief all-round the holiday came to an end, my sister and I looking slightly unkempt – with no parental reminder neither of us had changed our underwear all week. My long plaits had not been un-plaited since my mother had last done them, and soap and water had been completely disregarded. But my father looked as dapper as ever.

The taxi arrived to take us to the aerodrome and the sun was shining for the first time that week. The gloomy landlady had unbent enough to pat me on the head. We waved to the blonde waitress who was standing at the cafe door. She blew a kiss to my father who was intently looking the other way. The old lady with the umbrella waved her fist and muttered as we passed, her face full of hatred – I felt glad that we were not really Germans.

Leaving behind the dark, forbidding fortifications we once more took to the skies with our friendly pilot and headed for England. Back home everyone exclaimed with delight at the colour in my cheeks, which unfortunately turned out to be the first flush of Scarlet Fever.

My father never went on holiday again.

Money Talks

As my father's business expanded his clientele became more varied. His original customers, the coal miners of South Derbyshire, had been joined by highly paid production workers from the booming Coventry and Birmingham car plants. These new customers had ample wage packets that would have allowed them to explore the numerous High Street furniture shops that had opened up in every town. But they preferred to stick with the Tally Man distrusting the showy cheap multiple stores with their glib tongued salesmen.

The trust in my father was incredible. On his weekly rounds he would receive a wide range of orders for furniture and household goods that had been neither seen or selected, the customer relying totally on his judgement and honesty. His good taste was not always to be trusted, but no one ever complained. Their confidence was rarely misplaced; he would only deal in solid quality goods that would more than last a lifetime. The craftsmen-made sturdy furniture he sold is still in use in many homes. In the Tally Man's day no working-class home was complete without its walnut bedroom furniture resting on polished lino, or a plush, moquette, three-piece suite proudly displayed on an Axminster carpet square in a little used front room. My father's business fulfilled all these aspirations, and his calls to collect the weekly payments were accepted as part of the regular pattern of buying on credit. Alongside the rent man, insurance agent, and the clothing club, my father provided a service that allowed a little luxury into ordinary lives. He often said that the working man was the 'salt of the earth' and never looked for his clients away from working-class areas. He always treated them with the respect and courtesy that he expected in return.

After the Second World War ended the business developed even more. De-mobbed soldiers were coming back to wives and sweethearts and were glad to use the Tally Man's assistance to help furnish their homes. Orders came in faster than the manufacturer could supply. Utility furniture as it was called, was at that time the only available furniture. It was plain and serviceable, and in great demand. A sudden increase in pregnant customers created a need for cots and prams. My father sold the beautifully sprung 'Silver Cross' prams, always called the 'Rolls Royce' of baby carriages. It was one of these in the window display that attracted a shy young German girl into his shop. She was the bride of a local soldier, who had met and courted her in the ruins of Berlin. My father, always susceptible to a pretty blonde and moved by her nervousness and vulnerability, offered her a little discount, and easy weekly terms. Since arriving in England, she had met much hostility, both from her new in-laws and other shopkeepers, the recent war still fresh and raw in people's memories. She was reduced to tears by my father's attentive and kindly consideration and remained loyal to his business for many years to come, introducing many other German brides as customers.

In the Fifties his clientele became a little more exotic. When the first West Indians came to live and work in our small brewery town they were treated with some suspicion, if not a little fear by the local population. They were the first Black people to be seen on our streets. The Williams family who had recently arrived from Jamaica soon discovered my father's shop. His haphazard window dressing and disorganised shop floor obviously gave them nostalgic feelings of the markets back home, and after choosing their goods they acted accordingly. Whatever price my father quoted he found himself facing serious bargaining. After this first encounter, he quickly revised his sales techniques, mentally inflating his stock prices whenever Mr Williams introduced another West Indian family, and after intense lengthy exchanges honour would be satisfied on every side, the new family happy with their bargains, and my father content, having sold each item at its original price.

He became supplier of household furniture to most of the town's new immigrant work force. They came to trust him and value his opinions, often relying on his advice and help with personal problems. If anyone lagged behind with their weekly payments, Mr Williams and other prominent members of their community, would step in and chastise the culprit. Because of his business commitments my father had to decline the many wedding and party invitations that the West Indians showered on him, but he always sent a gift, having made a bulk purchase of colourful wool blankets especially for that purpose. At Christmas he was given bottles of Jamaican rum, which he never refused.

His business became even more multi-racial with the arrival of six young refugees from Budapest. He already had one young Hungarian on his books, Ivan, a coal miner, who had long been settled in his Derbyshire pit village, having fled Hungary at the end of the war. He had married a local girl, and they had furnished their pit cottage with the help of the Tally Man. In 1956 when news of the Hungarian uprising became known, Ivan had listened in anguish to the desperate pleas of his countrymen as they begged for help. He was frantic with worry when the radio appeals abruptly ended and longed for news of his elderly parents and three younger brothers. He was relieved a few days later to receive a telegram informing him that his brothers were safe. They were being held in a Red Cross camp in France and would be offered refugee status if he could offer them and their accompanying girlfriends a home.

The day of their arrival my father and I delivered extra beds to Ivan's small cottage, squeezing them into every spare space we could find. Our arrival coincided with the Red Cross van bearing its weary cargo of fugitives. We were swept up in the emotional greetings, kissed, hugged and invited inside to share wine and a meal.

In faltering English, the young men described the horror of their ordeal in Budapest. There had been a brief taste of freedom and jubilation, and then the feelings of hopelessness as the free world failed to respond to their frantic appeals for help. When the Russian tanks rolled in crushing the uprising they had fled. There had been no opportunity to say farewell to families or friends. Travelling only at night and sleeping in ditches by day they had managed to cross the border, claiming refugee status.

There were tears as these handsome young people told their stories, and the wine and the reminiscences were in full flow when my father and I left many hours later, very conscious of our good fortune to live in a free country.

The brothers married their girlfriends, settling in the same area as their older brother, all furnishing their new homes with the Tally Man's help. They all remained loyal to his business, and two decades later their children became customers too.

With the later advent of Asian immigration my father's business became truly international. Race, colour, or nationality found no prejudice with my father. He always said that money talks in any language.

Sabotage

Although my father was eccentric, we couldn't blame him for the 'Hanbury dump explosion', even though he happened to be in the vicinity at the time. Everyone in the area remembers where they were when it happened, like the day Kennedy was shot. Such was the force of the explosion every house for a radius of ten miles had cracked ceilings and walls, being accepted by building society surveys to this day as the results of the Hanbury dump explosion. At the time Hanbury was a small rural hamlet in Staffordshire, seemingly untouched by war, consisting of a few isolated farms and half a dozen cottages scattered around the village pub. The most exciting event in local memory being an escaping bull causing havoc one Sunday afternoon.

But unknown to all but the selected few, Hanbury's surrounding farmlands had been a wartime underground ammunition store. The area had been selected by the war office and the land requisitioned from the local farmers. Strict secrecy then surrounded its use, local gossip having it to be a training ground for spies, or possibly a government bolthole if Hitler invaded.

For fifty years the truth was never told, being classified as an official secret. But we all knew. At my young age I somehow thought my father might have been responsible, he having been in Hanbury village that day, and afterwards he said we couldn't talk about it because it was hush hush. I carried this worrying secret for years, not wanting to get my father into trouble.

Hanbury dump exploded early one autumn morning in 1944, believed to be sabotaged by Italian prisoners of war who worked as farm labourers in the area. The explosion caused widespread devastation over the countryside – whole farms disappeared into the bowels of the earth never to be seen again. Munition workers and countryfolk alike were buried alive. It was a tragic disaster. But it remained in war time Britain, a secret one.

My father had gone that day to Hanbury to look at some cattle a local farmer was selling. Standing in the farmyard when the massive explosion occurred, he was blasted across a field to be saved by the breadth and solid structure of a large haystack. He was lucky. The farmer, cattle, and farmhouse had been swallowed whole by the land they had been standing on.

Years later I learnt that my father had saved many lives, digging with his bare hands to recover buried workers from the dump.

There was a huge loss of life that day, followed by a total news blackout. Fifty years later it made little impact when the government of the day released some war-time secrets. The bygone tragedy only merited a couple of lines in national newspapers. Hanbury is now once again a tranquil hamlet. The huge craters caused by the explosion are now lush if oddly shaped meadows where cattle once again graze. No plaque marks the scene, but it remains a vivid memory to older local inhabitants who will never forget the day the dump exploded.

The Illuminations

The regular form of transport when I was a child was shanks' pony. Our farm track was almost a mile from the lane that led into the village where my sisters and I caught the school bus. In summer it was an idyllic walk, the path knee high with grass and wildflowers – we would saunter along making daisy chains or stealing purple blooms from the tall proud foxgloves that lined the hedge-growth, turning them into imaginary painted nails. We loitered deliberately, hoping the bus would have gone without us, but it never did.

My father took pity on us in the cold winter months and drove us to the end of the track, the five of us squashed into the back of his old pre-war van alongside the rattling milk churns. The van was not known for its starting powers on frosty mornings, and occasionally we were delivered to the bus on an equally ageing rusty tractor, all clinging precariously to my father as it rumbled up the pot holed lane. If this failed too, we would cadge lifts from the postman in his pony and trap, who swore and grumbled at us because he'd hoped for a cup of tea and a piece of cake. Our return from school coincided with my father's busy time in the milking sheds, and he worried about our lonely walk, particularly as it was often dark before we reached home. Being of an inventive and practical mind he soon came up with a solution, returning the very next market day with the promise of twelve so-called redundant telegraph poles, plus twelve arc lights. The war had only recently ended, and food was still rationed so we never queried these purchases or remarked about the two cured shoulders of ham that had mysteriously disappeared from the larder – my father being sensitive about his wheeling and dealing talents.

The poles and lights were set up at intervals alongside the farm track and then connected to a switch in the dairy. My father only had to look at his pocket watch to synchronise with the school bus' arrival and with one click the illuminations were on.

The first time they came on in their full glory it was wonderful – they shone so brightly and lit up the sky for miles. It was rumoured that people in the village panicked, thinking it was World War III. Some claimed that aliens were invading, and the local policeman got on his bicycle to go and investigate. All were reassured to find it was just another invention of my father's. He was well known to be eccentric and overprotective of his daughters.

The illuminations were not so popular as we got older. When walking back from the village dances arm in arm with local lads we would all blissfully saunter down the lane and turn into the farm track. Within seconds of feet touching our land a blaze of lights would appear, causing startled lads and rabbits to scatter in all directions, and in the distance the figure of my father with his shotgun and dogs, having guessed to the minute our arrival home. It did nothing at all for our love lives.

We all learnt to drive at seventeen and then my father's worries really started.

A Dog's Life

He came into our lives one wet Saturday evening. My father carried him in sheltered under his raincoat, tipped him out on to my lap and there he sat, a shivering damp ball of black wool with two sad, brown, almond shaped eyes staring up at me. He was a ten-week-old miniature poodle, given as payment for an outstanding debt. My father considered he had been short changed, but my sisters and I were ecstatic. We all loved and petted him, but from that very first evening all his loyalty and affection was given to my father.

As he grew, he was like a mischievous child, into everything and under everyone's feet. Although we had christened him 'Dandy', he only answered to my father calling him 'little black bugger', my father having no time for political correctness. We eventually shortened this to 'BB', it being considered more acceptable by all concerned.

He quickly knew the differences in my father's dress code - the early morning appearance of a business suit was enough for BB's tail to go down and for him to creep into his basket and sulk the day away. When my father changed into overalls it was a different BB that jumped about and barked with excitement. He followed him into the farmyard, strutting importantly as only poodles can, snapping bossily at the cows in the milking shed, scattering the hens who got in his way with a haughty flapping of his long ears and only forgetting his dignity for the time it took to chase the postman's van up the lane.

The days my father stayed on the farm were the happiest of BB's life. He loved following the tractor, and when my father was ploughing he would spend hours trotting up and down the field behind him, delicately stepping between the furrows and, when tired, was content to be picked up and sat on my father's lap until the work was done. My father often sang hymns to relieve the monotony of his chores and swore that BB joined in, barking in harmony, a strange sight for the passing rambler to observe: the big rugged farmer cradling the little dog, both singing and barking, oblivious to anyone.

BB was not allowed in the sitting-room, banished by my mother for scratching the furniture, but most evenings when my father was resting in his rocking chair and my mother dozing in front of the fire, he would slowly and stealthily edge his way into the room to sit at my father's side who, without stirring, would reach down and gently stroke the curly head resting at his feet. On one such evening he saved my parents from injury or worse, both having nodded off to sleep and unaware of a log falling from the grate which was smouldering on the carpet in front of them – BB frantically barked and pulled on my father's trouser legs to rouse him. After this incident my mother turned a blind eye to BB's crafty excursions into the sitting-room.

He loved company and was never happier than when all the family were at home, flitting from one to another, bestowing licks on his favoured humans, but always going back to sit at my father's feet. He became a nuisance when my sisters and I asked boyfriends back for a late-night coffee – he would fix them with a steely stare, growling softly if they moved an inch in our direction, once ripping the trousers of one who was brave enough to steal a goodnight kiss. He had been well tutored by my father.

The only bad days in his life were the visits he had to make to the dog clipper. He seemed to have a sixth sense when the morning of his appointment arrived, having to be dragged forcibly into the car, and burrowing his way under the driver's seat when the outskirts of the clipper's village were reached. Later, when collected, he would act affronted, indignant at his treatment, snubbing all our friendly overtures, but BB never stayed piqued for long and swaggering a little with his smart new haircut, his tail a perfect pom-pom, he would soon be back to his old self.

As BB matured, he had thoughts of romance and would often run away, racing across the fields in search of a girlfriend, quite prepared for a good telling off on his return, but hoping it would be worth it. One night he sped away on his usual quest, with my father grumbling about what he would do to him on his return, the grumbles covering his anxiety that BB had not yet returned, despite calling his name in every direction. It was getting dark when we saw the vet's car coming slowly down the drive. He got out of his car, ashen faced and carrying a small still body in his arms. It was BB, having ran his last romantic pursuit and getting his 'comeuppance' as my father had often said he would. The vet said he had been returning home from a late call when BB had run out of our lane like a streak of lightening, hitting the side of his car. He was sorry but there had been no chance of avoiding him. He then added in a reassuring voice, "The little fellow would not have suffered, it all happened so quickly."

My father said nothing. He took the lifeless body gently in his arms and walked away.

Later he wrapped BB in the blanket from his basket and carefully laid him to rest in a grave dug under the apple tree near the kitchen door.

My father brushed away his tears and gave his throat a loud clearing before turning to me, saying, "That's the last of that little black bugger."

The Money Bag

The brown leather Gladstone bag was as much part of my father's appearance as were the three-piece navy suits he always wore for business. Once a year he visited a local tailor and was measured for two identical suits. These were matched with blue and white striped shirts with stiff, white, detachable collars and, to complete the ensemble, a gold pocket watch and chain attached to his waistcoat front. He never veered from this mode of dress winter or summer, and although always smart, he never appeared dapper, a little too tall and rugged to ever give that impression. He more aptly fitted the overalls he wore when working around the farm. His one other eccentricity were the handmade, black, leather boots he always wore, crafted to his feet measurements. They were his only extravagance, once remarking that as a neglected child he had only worn-cast off footwear that rarely fitted.

The added sartorial touch of the brown leather bag was not a fashion statement, but a necessity. My father didn't believe in banks, along with income tax collectors and insurance companies – they were all untrustworthy in his opinion.

He carried large sums of money around with him at all times, packed tightly in the bag which was never far from sight or hand. We had a huge 'Chubb' safe cemented deep in the corner of our sitting-room, thinly disguised with an embroidered tablecloth thrown over it and a vase of flowers on top. This held the bulk of his money and valuables. It would have been a reckless thief who attempted a burglary, my father always having a loaded rifle within arm's-reach.

His unconventional way of dealing with financial matters could be a little unnerving for unsuspecting salesmen. On one occasion he left the farm still wearing his overalls and wellingtons, having taken a sudden whim to swap his troublesome car for a newer model. The superior minded sales manager looked on horrified at this definitely inferior being daring to sit in one of his highly polished new cars. "OUT!" he yelled at my father, forgetting for a second his superior manners. My father stayed where he was, slowly counting out a large amount of crinkly five-pound notes. He climbed out of the car as elegantly as was possible in wellington boots, placed the pile of notes on the shiny bonnet and said, "'I'll take it." The salesman changed colour and approached the cash and my father with care, obviously thinking he was dealing with an escaped lunatic.

This habit of carrying large sums of money around, plus his punctuality and the timing of his regular collecting rounds brought him some unwelcome attention. Twice he was attacked. The first time he was taken by surprise when leaving a customer's home. An assailant wielding a garden spade hit him from behind, repeatedly beating him about the head, but despite the damage inflicted, my father didn't let go of the money bag, and although the bag had permanent blood stains it, like he, survived to tell the tale.

The second assault came one dark winter's evening halfway through a busy collecting round. My father had become suspicious of two young men who seemed over interested in his route, and he was not taken unawares when the would-be thieves attacked. Using his money bag as a weapon he broke the nose of one and the arm of the other. He was seventy at the time, but a quick cup of tea at his next customer's house gave him the strength to finish his round.

I was once trusted to hold the bag, admittedly the house was on fire at the time. It was thrust into my hands whilst my father charged back into the smoke filled sitting room to empty the safe of its valuables. I guarded it with my life.

The bag remained in daily use until my father's death. It was looking worse for wear and shabby, but it had served him well.

I shed no tears at the funeral. They came afterwards when, going back to the farmhouse, I saw the empty discarded bag lying on the rubbish bin.

The Valley That Died

It was a relief when the final eviction notice came. For months the possibility of its arrival had overshadowed all our lives; the uncertainty had been difficult to live with. My father, like the rest of the valley's farmers, was feeling unsure, not knowing if he should make a start on the ploughing or purchase seed for the spring planting. We now had our answer. After years of anxiety and speculation a decision had at last been made. Our gentle rolling valley, home to at the most only half a dozen farming families, was soon to be submerged. The expanding urban spread of our nearest city needed water, understandable, but it was hard to accept that our quiet rural community would be sacrificed to give it to them.

The rumours had started four years earlier when two men in orange jackets were seen surveying the landscape. This quickly fuelled the idea that at long last the valley was to have a water supply, and ambitious gossips even suggested that the mains sewage might accompany it. Our remote district still relied on its wells and springs for water. As palatable as our cold crystal-clear water was, most of the valley's womenfolk dreamed of a bath night and washday free of the drudgery of carrying pails of water to heat in the old copper, and of the ultimate luxury of an indoor toilet. The farmers had some concern that the laying of pipes might disturb the early crops but were equally as enthusiastic as their wives. These happy thoughts lasted through another season but gradually abated when nothing more was heard, and no further sightings of orange-coated men reported.

The whole community was deeply shocked when early the following year every household received an official notification from the local water authority. The postman, who was running very late that morning, burst into our kitchen excitedly waving the letter in his hand, and not waiting for my father to open it, hastily divulged the contents. "They are flooding the valley. I'll be coming by boat soon," he cried. Ignoring the postman's obvious elation my father calmly sat down at the kitchen table, placed his reading glasses on the end of his nose and read out loud the formal looking letter. The water board after due consideration, wished to inform all concerned, that the land marked in red on the attached ordinance map was now under a potential compulsory requisition order. The scheme had government approval, but as two other sites were also under consideration no final ruling had yet been made on where the much-needed new reservoir would be located.

We all looked at the map on which our farmhouse and land was clearly outlined in red. My father carefully folded the letter, replaced it back in its envelope and put it behind the clock on the dresser where all our unimportant mail was put. It would lie there waiting to be thrown out when next my mother had a fit of tidying. He felt it was an empty threat. "The government's always having crackpot ideas, upsetting people, and nothing ever comes of it in the end." This was the general feeling amongst the valley people, and after the initial shock had worn off no more was said. Farmers continued with their seasonal work as usual, although a slight feeling of unease had crept into our lives.

The summer haymaking was in full swing when the next letter came. This one did cause concern. The Water Board were sending land valuers to visit each property and strongly advised the owners to have their own independent valuation done. This was beginning to sound serious; a meeting was called in the church hall for that night. The small room was crowded with anxious farming families.

My father was elected spokesman, having had previous experience with requisition when land he had owned in the next county was taken off him during the Second World War, good arable land it had been too. The Ministry of Defence had handed it back after the war had ended, but its green pastures were covered by great lengths of concrete runways which crossed the land in all directions. My father sold it on to a newly set up pig farmer, pigs not being averse to spending their days rooting around in broken concrete. His advice to the hastily called meeting was to stay put, keep calm, and put such an inflated value on to their properties that the Water Board would be frightened off.

A small group, my father included, was selected to approach the authorities to ask for a public inquiry to be held where all concerned could have their say. It was all too late, the plans were already signed and sealed, and no amount of pleas or even supportive media coverage could undo the inevitable. A promised parliamentary intercession by our local MP raised some hopes, but these were quickly dashed. Some of the valley's youngsters wanted to dump a load of manure on the Water Board's front doorstep, but were dissuaded by their elders who could see no sense in wasting good cow muck, the reality being that the needs and wishes of a few farmers in a small hamlet were totally outweighed by a growing city's demand for water.

Six months later the final eviction notices were hand delivered by Water Board officials, offering their sympathy but no reprieve. From that day the valley started to die. There were feelings of bewilderment and great sadness in our small community, but also much anger. Over the next few months we all came to a sense of reluctant acceptance, almost a period of mourning, with all having a deep awareness of our loss combined with apprehension for the future.

The valley started to look desolate as we lived out the final months of our expulsion. Cattle were sent off to market and not replaced, machinery rusted in leaking sheds and broken gates swayed in the wind. The very spirit of the valley seemed to have left, abandoning us to our fate. Many families had farmed these acres for generations. Young Tom Smitherd was unable to grasp that his newly inherited farm was soon to be taken from him, the land that his father and grandfather had lovingly tended was to lie dark and lost below depths of murky water. He declared he was glad his dad had died before the plans had become public knowledge, saying rather perversely, "it would have killed him you know." Peter Weston, our close neighbour, newly married with a baby already on the way, had decided from the start to move lock, stock and barrel, and emigrate to Canada. There had been Smitherds and Westons in the area for centuries and moss-covered crumbling gravestones in the tiny churchyard were the testimony to their hold in the valley. "The churchyard, what will happen to the graves?" an anxious widow asked. "My John's buried there and his dad before him." She was reassured that the Water Board had taken all these contingencies in hand when planning the valley's fate.

Once the valuations had been completed to everyone's satisfaction, generous compensation was paid, although how much money could you receive to make amends for the loss of your heritage and family history?

Removal vans were soon to be seen wending their way through our narrow lanes, an unusual sight in our valley. My father was the first to go. He had hoped to end his days on our peaceful farm, but he was realistic and more used to upheaval and travel than our neighbours. He was by this time nearing eighty and had decided to take things a little easier.

In my father's language this meant buying a smallholding of twenty acres nearer to town, and as expected, he was soon looking for further land to graze the young bullocks he had been unable to resist at the local cattle market.

We visited the valley just once more before it was flooded. It was a sombre sight, no smoking chimneys, the once lush pastures bereft of animals. The unforgettable memory was of the silence. Even the birds had left, and the blades of long grass seemed unmoved by the gentle breeze. The valley was dead.

The Boxing Day Hunt

The Boxing Day Meynell Hunt was a tradition long held in our county, a splendid sight when in full chase, galloping without hindrance across the Staffordshire countryside. That is, until my father purchased some extra land in the area called 'Upper Spinney Fields'. These fields were heavily wooded and a natural habitat for the fox, and the Meynell Hunt had crossed them freely for centuries.

That first time the Boxing Day Hunt rode in its full glory across my father's newly acquired land he was enraged. Hedges broken, gates damaged, and freshly ploughed fields trampled. Neighbouring landowners told him it was a waste of time protesting. The Boxing Day Meynell Hunt was the social event of the year for the local upper-class hunting set. This was no humdrum meeting, it was an elite gathering of the Shires nobility. Even kings had been known to ride with them.

My father was not impressed, and his anger smouldered over the next twelve months. Boxing Day arrived and with it came the expected frantic barking of the hounds and pounding of hooves as the hunt neared the entrance to 'Upper Spinney Fields'. This time he was waiting for them, standing in their track with a loaded shotgun in his hand, blocking the narrow bridle path that led on to his fields.

Lord Meynell, the hunt master, held up his whip to stay the hunt, and then used it to beckon my father forward. My father approached his lordship with his gun still cocked and saw a portly man whose face was nearly the colour of his scarlet coat and who, even on horseback, only matched my father's height. "I want you off my land," my father quietly said.

"My good man," replied Lord Meynell, "The hunt has crossed these fields for generations, and doubtless will do so long after you and I have gone to meet our maker. If a little damage occurs see my bailiff in the New Year and he will arrange for a couple of estate workers to come and put it right. Now come along good fellow, stop this ridiculous behaviour, and step out of my way. The mounts are getting cold and the hounds fretting."

He had chosen the wrong man. My father bowed to no one and, standing his ground, he raised his gun and fired two warning shots into the air, causing one aristocratic velvet clad lady to be unseated when her horse reared in fright, and presumably cleared the area of any lingering foxes.

The belligerent lord spurred forward his horse and shouting, "Tallyho," waved on the hunt, causing my father to jump out of the way for fear of being trampled on. This final indignity fuelled his rage. He angrily waved his fist, shouting to the hunt stragglers, "It's my land." Local onlookers were having fine entertainment, some enjoying my father's humiliation, but others secretly admiring his stand.

The anger still festered as the next Christmas approached. He had thought hard during the past year and conceived a dastardly plan. On Boxing Day morning, he was up at first light, placing chunks of fresh raw meat along the hedge bottoms in every corner of Upper Spinney Fields. And this time he stood back in satisfaction as the hunt surged in from the narrow entrance and headed for the spinneys. The hungry hounds, smelling an early breakfast, broke free from their pack, splitting up and speeding off in all directions. The huntsmen were baffled, circling the field, imagining it to be overrun with foxes. My father watched this chaos with a broad smile on his face. But seconds later the hounds' master arrived on the scene. Taking in the situation at a glance and with two sharp whistles he had the hounds reformed in their pack, some still chewing on their unexpected treat.

My father's plan had not entirely succeeded, despite the mayhem caused. The hunt had still survived to plague him another day. Refusing to lose the battle, he put his drastic final solution in hand. During the early autumn of the following year he hired a digger and tore up the ancient spinneys. The foxes moved on.

It took one more Boxing Day for the hunt to realise that both spinneys and foxes had gone. In bewilderment, hunters and hounds surveyed the desolate spinney fields then moved dejectedly on. With no quarry to pursue they had to find other woodlands to hunt.

My father had won his battle but lost our beautiful spinneys. The Meynell Hunt never crossed our land again and eventually my father replanted one small spinney, now grown to a little of its former glory. But the foxes never returned.

The Mistress

I first realised that my father had a mistress when I was just turned twelve. I was sent up to the top fields where he was assumed to be ploughing that day. My task was to deliver his forgotten sandwiches and flask of tea. I arrived at the fields to find the tractor silent and unmoved and no sign of my father. I circled the large haystack in the corner of the field, calling him, thinking he might be playing a trick on me.

Then I saw them, lying on the grass, kissing and cuddling. At first, I could only register surprise that She should be there, She being one of my father's employees from his business in town and who didn't belong to our life on the farm. My second thought was what white legs she had, never having seen her before without stockings on, and with her skirt up to her waist.

I had enough wit to turn and sidle back round the haystack into the hedge bottom and, keeping out of sight, crawled along the ditch into the next field, and then on my feet, running as fast as I could back home. My father went without his lunch that day.

She started gradually to intrude on our lives. My father gave her a small car, ostensibly to help in the business and to allow her to reach the farm twice a week to assist with household chores.

She was a small plump woman, smartly dressed, permed and perfumed, and when she was around, the click of her high heels and the rattle of her many bracelets always preceded her into the room.

She tried to make friends with us all, and succeeded with my sisters: varnishing their nails, curling their hair, sometimes taking them home with her for the day, her husband being a long-distance lorry driver who was often away. But I held back, not wanting her offers of friendship. She gave us all gifts and I refused mine, causing my mother to rebuke me for my rudeness.

She used to slyly probe my mother's housekeeping bills and then report to my father on any extravagances, the cause of many matrimonial rows.

Strange now, to recall that everyone called her June, but she always remained just She to me. My father's relationship with her continued unrecognised as such, for another five years.

I realised that my father was a coward with women when he gave me the responsibility of breaking off the long association they had shared. She had been away on holiday and returned to work to be met by me at the office door who, following my father's instructions, gave her one month's wages and her cards, saying, "My father doesn't want to see you anymore. You're sacked." Her face crumbled and tears came. It should have been my finest hour, but I felt sorry for her in the end. As time passed others followed in her steps, but none ever so serious or as long lasting as She. And if my mother knew she never acknowledged it.

In his later years my father's affairs slowed down, a combination of his lessening appetites, and the realisation that we girls were growing up and he didn't want to lose our respect.

When my father died many of the female mourners at his funeral had probably been a little closer to him then they should have been. And later at the graveside a small elderly lady caught my eye. I recognised her, looking old and frail, but still powdered and perfumed and keeping up her appearance. She had come to pay her respects. Perhaps She had really loved him after all. I nodded my head in recognition. She nodded back. Before leaving, she placed one white rose on the coffin and then, half turning at the church gate, she winked at me knowing full well what I had seen all those years ago, and as if thanking me for keeping it secret.

It was no hardship because I loved him too and had kept all his secrets well.

A Family Reunion

My father was an atheist and other than a brief flirtation with the 'Holy Rollers' during his misspent youth in Canada, had remained so all his life. The family were surprised when in his later years he decided he would like to be buried in the village churchyard.

On his death we complied with his wishes, arranging for a short church service followed by his internment in what must be one of the most beautiful and peaceful burial grounds in the country. Although, the thought did cross our minds that it might be less tranquil after my father's burial, his plot lying between the recently deceased blacksmith with whom he'd had a long-standing feud and a neighbouring farmer whom he'd threatened to shoot if he allowed his cattle to stray once more on our land. Fortunately, nature had also removed him before my father could carry out this threat.

Family attendance at the funeral was small, limited to my mother, four sisters and myself, my father having broken ties with his relatives half a century earlier, and my mother's family never quite forgiving her for marrying a man old enough to be her father. And of course, mine and my sisters' assorted husbands didn't really count, having only been tolerated by my father in his lifetime. The half mile drive to the church was lined by local people, "Just checking he's really gone," remarked one of the husbands.

"He'll be back for some discount."

"We should have used the Co-op and got some stamps," said another. As we approached the church, we were all in fits of laughter, very close to tears.

The vicar, with a sombre face, started the service talking of the virtues my father had possessed and of his wonderful strength of character. Unfortunately, he triggered a memory I had of many years before when this same vicar had gone into town to choose a three piece suite from our furniture store, for his newly built vicarage, and having opted for the most expensive one on display, asked my father if he would contribute the cost as a gift to the church. Only a few months earlier his wife had refused to allow me into the Brownie pack because my family were not churchgoers. My father had all but booted him out of the door. And here he was, conducting the funeral service. Some might say it was the ultimate act of forgiveness, but I had the feeling that if he became too fulsome, the coffin lid would fly off and my father would rise up and punch him. The service continued with no such incident, and we sang 'Plough the Fields and Scatter the Good Seed on the Land', a hymn much loved by my father, obviously a remnant of his 'Holy Roller' days.

There was a feeling of suppressed happiness, pain at his loss, but so glad that he had died as he had wanted, with his boots on, ploughing one last straight furrow, then steering his tractor neatly into the hedge when the first chest pain hit. A perfect ending for a man who was never perfect, but who had made his mark.

All through the service two tall strangers had stood at the rear of the church, looking uncomfortable and yet familiar. They followed the family to the graveside, standing back a little, their heads bowed with respect. They came on to the farmhouse for refreshments, none of us liking to ask who they were. They eventually introduced themselves using my father's surname as their own. I think we had all guessed their identity before they said anything more. The elder of the two was my father's double.

They were both his sons, born in a relationship before he married my mother. We had never heard a whisper about them before, or they of us, and although my father had fed, clothed and educated them, he had never until this day owned them. He had left instructions with his solicitor to inform them of his death and request their attendance at his funeral. Typical of him to play the last card. I felt sure that wherever he was he would be enjoying the drama of this unforeseen family reunion.

Rita Jerram

Rita Jerram was born in 1938 in Staffordshire, the second of five daughters. At the age of 15 she was diagnosed with Tuberculosis following a rapid physical decline caused by anorexia. She was admitted to Outwoods Sanatorium for treatment and spent a year on an adult ward, during which she developed a love of literature and a gratitude for life, having witnessed the death of several of the women she had come to regard as her family. After her recovery, in 1957 she travelled to Australia alone, leaving behind her distraught parents who never quite understood why she was not content to settle down and conform to 1950s small town expectations.

Always a restless spirit with no outlet for her intelligence and creativity, Rita tried many different jobs, including working as a nanny in Paris and completing a year of nursing training. She returned to Burton on Trent in 1963, where she married. Two sons and a daughter were born between 1964 and 1969.

In 1970 Rita emigrated with her family to Australia, moving on to the Fiji Islands in 1972, where she experienced Hurricane Bebe. The following year the family travelled to New Zealand. Throughout this period Rita wrote to her parents and sisters, who eagerly awaited each letter, entertained by her gift for storytelling.

In 1974 Rita and her family returned to England, living first in Bognor Regis, and then moving to Harrogate. After her divorce in the 1990s, she tried various jobs, including being a family aide for social services, a housing association warden and a crisis call responder. In 1997 she moved to York where she undertook several creative writing classes.

Initially doubting her ability, Rita's confidence increased as her work was clearly enjoyed by others. She began to write in every spare moment, feeling she had finally found the creative fulfilment that had been missing from her life. While a member of a group led by Pauline Kirk (editor of Fighting Cock Press) she shared the stories she was writing, based on her Grandmother's journal. The interest they aroused led in 2015 to the joint publication of *Tales From A Prairie Journal* by Stairwell Books and Fighting Cock Press. This was followed by *A Shadow In My Life* in 2017.

On the 29 March 2018, Rita died, aged 80, in St Leonard's Hospice, York, leaving many unpublished stories, and the manuscript of *The Tally Man*.

Other biographies, memoires and history available from Stairwell Books and Fighting Cock Press

The Great Billy Butlin Race	Robin Richards
Mistress	Lorraine White
The Tao of Revolution	Chris Taylor
Margaret Clitherow	John and Wendy Rayne-Davis
Serpent Child	Pat Riley
Looking for Githa	Patricia Riley
The Martyrdoms at Clifford's Tower 1190 and 1537	John Rayne-Davis
A Shadow in My Life	Rita Jerram
Thinking of You Always	Lewis Hill
Tales from a Prairie Journal	Rita Jerram

For further information please contact rose@stairwellbooks.com

www.stairwellbooks.co.uk
@stairwellbooks

www.ingramcontent.com/pod-product-compliance
Lightning Source LLC
Chambersburg PA
CBHW020959090426
42736CB00010B/1383